You Are Highly Favored

You Are Highly Favored

Reflections from the Nativity to Encourage Your Faith

A 25 Day Christmas Devotional

L. M. TIMPANO

YOU ARE HIGHLY FAVORED

Reflections from the Nativity to Encourage Your Faith

Copyright © 2016 by Lacy M. Timpano

First Edition: November 2015

Second Edition: November 2016

Printed by CreateSpace

Unless otherwise indicated, scripture quotations are from the ESV® Bible (The Holy Bible, English Standard Version®), copyright © 2001 by Crossway, a publishing ministry of Good News Publishers. Used by permission. All rights reserved.

Scripture quotations marked (NASB) are taken from the New American Standard Bible®, Copyright © 1960, 1962, 1963, 1968, 1971, 1972, 1973, 1975, 1977, 1995 by The Lockman Foundation. Used by permission. (www.Lockman.org)

Scripture quotations marked (NIV) are taken from the Holy Bible, New International Version®, NIV®. Copyright © 1973, 1978, 1984, 2011 by Biblica, Inc.™ Used by permission of Zondervan. All rights reserved worldwide. www.zondervan.com The "NIV" and "New International Version" are trademarks registered in the United States Patent and Trademark Office by Biblica, Inc.™

Scripture quotations marked (NKJV) are taken from the New King James Version®. Copyright © 1982 by Thomas Nelson. Used by permission. All rights reserved.

ISBN-13: 987-1534683761
ISBN-10: 1534683763

Printed in the United States of America

Contents

"Be strong and courageous. Do not be afraid... for the Lord your God goes with you..."

- DEUTERONOMY 31:6

Preface

Not long after being married, my husband and I had a number of years in which we really struggled financially when the holiday season rolled around. I always loved the joy of the season, but felt the weight of frustration from not being able to afford much for gifts for our families. I hated the pressure, the crunch, and the heightened awareness it gave me of the giant black hole of financial lack that seemed to be eating up our lives. We walked away from Christmas, more often than not, with some bit of extra acquired debt, and spent the rest of the year trying to shed it off like unwanted holiday pounds.

I remember one year taking a stroll down the path near my family's house. It was a blustery and cold day in early December, in spite of the sunny sky. The dead leaves were being tossed around by the crisp breeze, and it felt good to be outside. My husband, John, and I had just finished watching the movie *The Nativity Story*, as we do every year. While I have always enjoyed watching it, it struck a deep chord in me that year, and we talked about it as we walked.

I felt incredibly moved by the account of Mary and Joseph, and the journey they took. They were so ordinary, their lives so humble. Situationally they seemed anything but blessed, and yet God said they were highly favored. As I meditated on this, I began to evaluate my understanding of God's favor. I think it rang true with me that December especially, because of the feelings I was struggling with over the loss and lack in our lives. I felt empty and obscure, and would often ask John, "If God loves me, then where is his favor in my life?"

When I watched *The Nativity Story* afresh that winter, I saw so much more in it than I ever did before. It is a story filled with trust. It is a story about great courage. It is a story about two people completely misunderstood by the people around them, living in obscure circumstances, walking by faith regardless of what fear or lack they may have had. They were blessed, and highly favored.

I wrote this devotion with the purpose of encouraging those who may be discouraged at the struggles in which they may be finding themselves. Christmas can be, no matter what our financial situation, a time for comfort and joy, a time for generosity, and a time for connecting with the heart of God as we remember not only the great gift He gave us, but the awe-inspiring manner in which that gift was given. If you have been struggling with identifying God's grace and favor in your life, then I invite you to come with me and take a fresh look at what it really means to be blessed and highly favored.

December 1st

PREPARE HIM ROOM

Joy to the world, the Lord is come!
Let earth receive her king;
Let every heart prepare him room,
and heaven and nature sing...

- ISAAC WATTS

The age old hymn says it well, and echoes the heart of advent, the season leading up to Christmas. There is a preparation that needs to be made in each of us; decluttering the space in our hearts, tossing out the old ways of thinking, getting rid of unhealthy mindsets, nudging over our self-centeredness, and making room for Christ the King to come center. He wants to come and fill up that space, every crack and crevice, with His love, favor, and grace. He wants us to encounter Him, and He is beckoning our hearts through the season of Christmas.

Each year we have the opportunity to look with fresh eyes at the life-changing mystery of not only how He came, but why He came. It is the greatest love story ever told. It is the story of majesty, and humility; how God clothed Himself in human flesh, and ransomed us from our sin. The greatest of kings was born in the lowliest of places. He could have been born in a palace, amongst royalty and riches, but He chose instead to come into this world in the most humble of ways. There is a reason why God came the way He did; it was part of His perfectly crafted story, just like His plan to redeem you and me. He came as our humble king, demonstrating that He would go to whatever lengths necessary to bring us back to Himself.

Wrapped up in all the traditions of the season, sometimes we forget that Jesus' birth is something that really happened. As we go along, doing our Christmas shopping, sending and receiving Christmas cards, giving Christmas gifts, and singing Christmas carols, we forget that it is all more than just a story; we forget that Jesus really came. We have made the image of the nativity so sweet and mild that God's majesty often gets left out, and we lose the sense of His greatness. If we really stop to think about the manner in which Jesus was born, and the extravagance of His mission, it should leave us completely blown away. May we prepare our hearts to encounter God in a new way this Christmas, to be reminded of the splendor of history past, and what that means for our present and our future. Let's make room to receive our king.

ZECHARIAH 9:9 NASB

Rejoice greatly, O daughter of Zion! Shout in triumph, O daughter of Jerusalem! Behold, your king is coming to you; He is just and endowed with salvation, humble, and mounted on a donkey, even on a colt, the foal of a donkey.

December 2nd

WHAT IS FAVOR?

PROVERBS 16:15
In the light of a king's face there is life, and his favor is like the clouds that bring the spring rain.

If I asked you today, "*What does it mean to have favor?*"…what would you answer? I used to think of people who had favor as having success, power, or wealth. Or that to have favor meant to get what you wanted. For things to be easy, to be unhindered. The word favor itself means goodwill, acceptance, an attitude of approval or liking. Favor is an act of kindness beyond what is due. It means demonstrated delight. Interestingly enough, the Greek word for favor, *charis*, is also translated as grace. Grace and favor are deeply intertwined. Grace is, after all, unmerited favor.

These descriptions are so different from what I think

comes to mind for most of us when we hear the word favor. When I used to look at my own life, I felt that because we were struggling in many areas — progress forward in jobs, finances, infertility — we must have very little favor. I even felt like God was against me, but that couldn't have been further from the truth. The truth is that when we come to salvation through the blood of Jesus, we are granted access to the Father and His throne of grace. His favor is extended to us, His demonstrated delight. *His favor is like the clouds that bring the spring rain.*

When we struggle it does not mean that God is not for us. It took me a long time to grasp that favor is not about success. Favor is about the light of the King's face shining with love and approval upon us, and we have that through Jesus Christ. It's already ours! We always favor those we love, and God's love for us is greater than we could ever grasp. So is His favor.

If you have a relationship with Jesus Christ, God delights in you and you have His favor. It is not something we earn or un-earn. Like grace, it is a gift. We may not always feel it, sense it, or see it visibly at work in our lives, but His favor always abides with His presence. Where He is, all that He is is there with Him. Life is not always easy, and we must work through the consequences of our choices at times. We don't always know the rhyme or the reason, but difficult times do not mean that God is not for us. He is often working in ways unseen, ways which are often only afterward revealed. Our hearts of belief can usher in God's presence when we let His will be done, and with it comes all the absolutes of who God is, in His abundant goodness and favor.

LUKE 1:28 NIV

And the angel went to her and said, "Greetings, you who are highly favored! The Lord is with you."

December 3rd

LESSONS FROM THE NATIVITY

LUKE 1:30-31
And the angel said to her, "Don't be afraid, Mary, for you have found favor with God. And behold, you will conceive in your womb and bear a son, and you shall call his name Jesus."

Mary and Joseph were just ordinary people, from the obscure Galilean town of Nazareth. God took perhaps the most unlikely of people, from the most unlikely of places, and used them to carry forth His plan and make a way for the greatest of gifts to come to mankind. It is an incredible story when you stop and really look at it. Don't let the familiarity of it steal the awe. Take a step back if you need to, and look at it with fresh eyes.

I love the nativity story because it is such a clear reminder that God's call on our lives isn't always easy.

It can be hard, even humbling. Favor does not mean our journey will always be easy, or that our calling will be without struggles. We can be in a difficult situation, and still be right in the middle of God's perfect will. Difficulties and struggles do not mean that God is not near, or that He is not for us. Mary and Joseph walked a road that was full of social taboos, misunderstanding, and even physically very difficult. It was a monumental destiny that changed everything they knew about their lives, and they embraced it with humble and thankful hearts of faith.

It is incredibly easy to disqualify ourselves and get lost in the humdrum of everyday life. It is easy to feel obscure in the ordinary. But what I pull from this account in the Bible is that just because life is tough, even humbling, it doesn't mean that God is not in our story. The quote from Oscar Isaac says it well, "God made Himself flesh in the most humble of ways with the most humble people. Jesus was not born to kings or wealthy people but to Mary and Joseph, poor but righteous." There is deep purpose in why God orchestrated it this way. I believe that God wanted to speak to people, to reach down and let us know that no matter who you are, no matter what situation you may find yourself in, that our Father is a humble king, and He is with the humble.

Just because you have struggles and hardship does not

mean that you do not have God's favor. We can have God's favor and still be poor. We can have God's favor and be misunderstood. Favor is not about possessions or position, it is about the heart. What we see through the nativity story is a shining example of how God looks at the heart, not at the situation. He looked on Mary and called her blessed and favored. Their journey was anything but easy, yet it is a testament that an ordinary life is not necessarily a life unmarked by favor, even one that faces great difficulties.

December 4th

STEWARDING FAVOR

LUKE 2:52
And Jesus increased in wisdom and in stature and in favor with God and man.

Favor is truly an incredible, though often mis-understood gift. It is not given, only to be left dormant, tucked away on a shelf or hidden in a pocket — it is meant to be sown with purpose, to be cultivated, to *grow*. Even Jesus Himself grew in favor, and we each have the opportunity to do the same. To not do so would be to stop short of so many blessings, for favor is like a gateway through which God ushers in all the fullness of who He is and what He has for us, because favor is about *fullness*.

Let's take a look the parable of the talents, from Matthew 25:14-30 (go ahead and read that now if you aren't already familiar with it). I love this parable because it demonstrates for us what it means to be good stewards. Stewarding is all about taking care of whatever you have, and to whatever measure has been given to you, being faithful to do something with it. In the parable the master praises each steward, from great to small, until he gets to the steward that did nothing with his talent. He was so overcome by the fear of failure that he did nothing. Instead, he buried his talent and just hoped for the best.

In the same way, many of us move through life paralyzed by fear. We've been given this incredible gift of favor, and yet we are too afraid to do anything with it. Like the steward who buried his talent, favor does us little good if we do nothing with it. We can, however, steward favor by being faithful with what we already have.

When we steward favor well, it cultivates something in us, in our character and who we are. It shapes us and makes us ready, and prepares us to say yes to God's call on our lives. We cannot grow in favor without it transforming who we are. Proverbs 8 says that by seeking wisdom and understanding, we find life and get favor from God. James 4:6 says, "God opposes the proud, but gives grace to the humble." That word for grace is *charis* — meaning favor comes when we walk in humility. Proverbs 3:3-4 says that we find favor when we hold fast to love and faithfulness.

Favor, indeed, does not come without it changing who we are for the better.

Lets change our thinking of what favor is all about. God does not give us favor to be like spoiled children, but to transform us, and make us ready to be who He has called us to be. His gifts and His callings are so good, and big and full of blessings, lets not sell ourselves short because we are afraid! History is hinging on our response. What kind of stewards will we be?

MATTHEW 25:21

His master said to him, "Well done, good and faithful servant. You have been faithful over a little; I will set you over much. Enter into the joy of your master."

December 5ᵗʰ

HEARTS PREPARED FOR DESTINY

MATTHEW 1:24
When Joseph awoke from his sleep, he did as the angel of the Lord had commanded him: he took his wife.

LUKE 1:38
And Mary said, "Behold, I am the servant of the Lord; let it be done unto me according to your word."

One of the biggest questions I have asked myself as I have looked at the lives of Mary and Joseph is this: what made their hearts ready to receive their destiny with such faith, humility, and trust? They were just ordinary people, from an ordinary town, and yet their hearts responded with such unwavering faith. They both were even afraid. These weren't super-humans that God had chosen, they were just like you and me, with questions and fears and choices to sort through. It brings the story down to earth, when you really stop to look at all the human aspects about how God became flesh.

In Matthew 1:19 the Bible calls Joseph a just man, and says that he was unwilling to put Mary to shame. Of Mary, we see her response of faith to the angel in Luke 1. She recognized herself as God's servant. From looking at the accounts of these two, from both Matthew and Luke, we see that Mary and Joseph were righteous, humble, and gracious people who had ears to hear, and hearts of faith to respond with obedience to God's call on their lives. From the humility, wisdom, grace and faithfulness we see in these two, we can see the fruit of what they had been cultivating in their hearts all along. They were indeed already stewarding favor and grace in their lives, so it is no surprise that they were ready for God's call, however difficult it was.

They were ready because their hearts were prepared. They were ready because they understood grace. They were ready because they knew who they were, and from that foundation of identity, they were able to embrace the difficult, yet blessed calling before them. Where there is identity there is no shame. You can see how the angel of the Lord (in Luke 1:28) encouraged

Mary in this when he said, "You are highly favored!" "The Lord is with you." These statements were intended to raise her sense of value in the Lord. God's presence is near what He delights in. He is, after all, Emmanuel, God with us.

God has incredible delight in us. We too, can be ready to respond to whatever God's call is for our lives, but our hearts have to be prepared to receive more favor. Are you ready? Are you really ready to count the cost? All those characteristics that made Mary's and Joseph's hearts ready to respond the way they did, began growing long before the day the angel came. It is a wonderful thing to know God, and to know who we are in Him. Without shame, without fear, because you know that God's presence is with you, and His delight is for you.

December 6th

TRUSTING WHEN
WE DON'T UNDERSTAND

PROVERBS 3:5-6 NKJV
Trust in the Lord with all your heart, and lean not on your own understanding; In all your ways acknowledge Him, and He shall direct your paths.

One of the greatest challenges to our faith is to trust when we do not understand. Being understood makes us feel valued, it makes us feel connected. I think one of the reasons we struggle to trust God when we don't understand is because we do not feel connected. At heart, we are really questioning who God is. Is He faithful? Is He trustworthy? Does He really have my best interests in mind? We question who God is, and we question the value of who we are to Him.

I believe this is one of the reasons that God allows

difficulties to come into our lives. They are not meant to push us away from God and into the isolation of mistrust. They are meant to push us towards Him, and to help build in us a strong foundation of identity and intimacy. If there is one thing that is without question, it is our value to Him. The devil will do whatever he can to lie to you and get you to believe otherwise, because the strength of knowing your value in Christ is powerful! When we know our value in Christ it helps us to feel connect to God's heart through times when we don't understand. It becomes like an anchor, holding us steady through the tossing of the storm.

Mary knew who she was. She declared herself the servant of the Lord. She was declaring her trust in God in spite of her understanding. When life is full of troubles we too have the opportunity to declare our trust in God, even if we don't understand. This is the kind of faith that moves mountains. Mountains represent something that stands in our way, and faith is how we will get through them. We walk by faith and not by sight. It is not about understanding; it is about putting our faith in God when we can't see. Faith is the substance of things hoped for, the evidence of things not yet seen. Mary was putting her faith in the unseen promise that was hidden in her womb, the very substance of what Israel was hoping for.

It takes faith to lean on God and to trust when we do not understand. We cannot trust with just a portion, we must trust with our whole being. With *all* of our hearts. We can't always understand the circumstances around us, but we can know the value of who we are in Christ, and who He is. When we know that God is always trustworthy, and that He always has the best in mind for us, it will release us to be at peace and to lean upon Him, even when we can't comprehend what is going on around us. What is happening on the outside won't matter so much when we are anchored on the inside.

December 7th

BEING OBEDIENT WHEN
OTHERS DON'T UNDERSTAND

LUKE 1:35

*And the angel answered her, "The Holy Spirit will
come upon you, and the power of the Most High
will overshadow you; therefore the child to be born
will be called holy—the Son of God."*

Put yourself in Mary's shoes for a moment. A virgin,
engaged to be married, found to be pregnant by
the Holy Spirit. Could you imagine trying to break
the news to your family, and how they would have
reacted? Could you imagine telling your betrothed? If
you went to your friends today and told them what
Mary would have said to hers, what would they say
to you? Step into Joseph's shoes. A man with a good
heart, who had lived righteously, and whose fiancé was
found to be pregnant with a child that was not his.

How do you think the people around him looked at him after they heard the news? It would have appeared to be downright scandalous, and yet God was right in the middle of it, His perfect plan set in motion. Really, stop and take a moment to think about what it would have been like to be them. It is remarkable the way their hearts trusted, when you consider the amount of misunderstanding they had to face.

This is a great example for us, that sometimes God's call on our lives might seem so outside the box to the people around us that they do not understand. It is very hard when the people you love don't understand you, and an even more difficult thing to be misunderstood. When we don't feel known by those around us, we feel lonely and isolated. I think John Maxwell put it perfectly when he said, "Loneliness is not the absence of faces, but the absence of intimacy." So what do we do if we're stuck in the place of choosing between being obedient to God and being understood by others? We crave intimacy, and rightly so; intimacy is the answer. There is only one person in our lives who deserves to be king of our hearts, and that is Jesus. The priority of the people in our lives is revealed by those we seek to know and be known by the most. If you feel the tug of pleasing people pulling you to make decisions that go against what you know God has asked you to do, you have to ask yourself whose company is most important to you?

Mary and Joseph responded with a resounding yes to God's call, even in the face of opposition and great misunderstanding. They were willing to be looked down on, shunned, and mislabeled. They were so connected with the mission of heaven that it superseded what would have been a difficult burden to bear. What an amazing destiny they would have missed out on if they had been too afraid of what other people thought rather than respond to God's call! Let's respond to God with a resounding *yes* today, too.

December 8th

WHEN WE MESS THINGS UP

LUKE 1:5-7

*In the days of Herod, king of Judea, there was a
priest named Zechariah, of the division of Abijah.
And he had a wife from the daughters of Aaron,
and her name was Elizabeth. And they were both
righteous before God, walking blamelessly in all the
commandments and statutes of the Lord. But they
had no child, because Elizabeth was barren, and
both were advanced in years.*

LUKE 1:18-20

*And Zechariah said to the angel, "How shall I know
this? For I am an old man, and my wife is advanced
in years." And the angel answered him, "I am
Gabriel. I stand in the presence of God, and I was
sent to speak to you and to bring you this good news.
And behold, you will be silent and unable to speak*

until the day that these things take place, because you did not believe my words, which will be fulfilled in their time."

What a bitter sting for Zechariah, to have been given such great news, and to have ruined it by his unbelief. Really, can you imagine having waited years, to have been past all hope for a child, for such a great desire to have come and gone and for an angel to come to you and say, "Congrats, you're gonna have a son and he's going to be awesome!" I can practically see his jaw hit the floor. Imagine, after the shock of the news, Zechariah leaving the temple and going to his wife, and not being able to say *anything*. Have you ever had a secret that was so good, you wanted to burst inside from having to hold it in? I can only imagine how Zechariah must have felt; the tension between the excitement of the news, and perhaps the remorse of his response.

The Bible says that Zechariah was righteous before God, and blameless, and even still he struggled in his faith. What a testament to the graciousness of God, that even though Zechariah made a mistake, God did not withhold His promise or favor from him. It did not change God's mind about how He viewed or loved him or His plan for him. I love reading about Mary and Joseph, because their obedient faith is so inspiring, but it is also wonderful to have an example before us of God working His plan even through failure. We all make mistakes, we don't always respond the way we should, but God is faithful to not only work His good through it, but work His good *in* us. It is reassuring to know that we serve a good God who can and will work His favor in our lives even when we mess things up. Thank you Jesus!

LUKE 1:13

But the angel said to him, "Do not be afraid, Zechariah, for your prayer has been heard, and your wife Elizabeth will bear you a son, and you shall call his name John."

December 9th

GOD'S TIMING IS PERFECT

MATTHEW 1:18
Now the birth of Jesus Christ took place in this way. When his mother Mary had been betrothed to Joseph, before they came together she was found to be with child from the Holy Spirit.

It was a perfect July afternoon in the High Sierras as John and I were making our way down to the valley floor of Yosemite National Park. The thrill in the air was palpable, and I just knew it was coming; I knew he was going to propose that day, and he did. It remains one of the best days of my life; the moments and memories of it linger vividly in my mind. The warm light cascading through the trees from the late afternoon sun, the rush of water, the cool breeze, the open air, the stunning view of Half Dome. Love swelled in our hearts and the world was at our fingertips.

That season of engagement was such a special one, so when I stop and read over Mary and Joseph's story once more, it really speaks to me in a new way. There they were, betrothed, pledged to be married. It would have been a thrilling time for them, yet Mary is found to be with child from the Holy Spirit. In some ways, God's plan could have felt very much like bad timing. It completely disrupted their plans, and yet it bears beautiful testimony to the level of trust that Mary and Joseph had in God. Even in the midst of their betrothal they were willing to be vessels of God's glorious plan, and through their responsive faith they got to bear the greatest of all gifts.

Even for Zechariah and Elizabeth, things seemed to be too late. They were long gone out of childbearing years, and yet hope came to them at the most unlikely time. For Mary and Joseph, things seemed to be happening too soon. God's promise was coming to Israel, for these two people, in a way that would turn their world upside down. Zechariah responded with doubt, Mary and Joseph with faith, yet God came knocking just the same with plans that were greater than any of them could have imagined. They were big, good, awesome plans, and they came right on time.

Things happen that we don't always understand. They

seem out of place, in the wrong time, and yet they are happening just the same. What we do and how our hearts respond when we find ourselves in those moments is more important. Disruption isn't always a bad thing. Sometimes it can be God's greatest compassion and love for us to bring big changes, even if the timing seems strange. He sees the big picture. He is the great conductor, and His timing is perfect. Nothing is outside the spectrum of God's control. The timing may not always make sense, but His plan for us is always good. I am very thankful for such a testimony laid before us, that sometimes what seems like bad timing can actually be perfect timing, because it is God's timing.

December 10th

DON'T LIVE FROM FEAR

MATTHEW 2:1-3

Now after Jesus was born in Bethlehem of Judea in the days of Herod the king, behold, wise men from the east came to Jerusalem, saying, "Where is he who has been born king of the Jews? For we saw his star when it rose and have come to worship him." When Herod the king heard this, he was troubled, and all Jerusalem with him.

Herod. Now there's a character we don't typically see focused on. He may not be the most likely person, but I think we might be surprised how much we can learn from him. In Herod we see what happens when we respond to fear and let it rule the choices we make. Fear is one of the greatest forces that will drive a wedge between us and God, and wreak havoc on the decisions we make. If there is one thing we can see woven throughout the story of Jesus' birth, it is that trust is a huge part of saying yes to God and walking in His favor. Zechariah, Joseph, Mary and Herod all found themselves in similar circumstances. They were troubled at the news that came to them, perplexed, even afraid, and they each made choices that played out how they responded to that fear, and it became part of history.

For Herod, he allowed himself to be ruled by his fear. When he heard from the magi about the king who had been born, he was deeply troubled. He tried to trick the magi into finding where Jesus had been born, and to report back to him so that he could "worship him" too. Nice try, Herod. When he realized that the magi had outsmarted him, he became furious, and ordered that all baby boys two years old and younger be killed. Herod was so overcome by fear that he tried to trick the wise, and murdered the innocent.

Herod was afraid of someone else's favor; a baby, born king of the Jews. He was afraid of losing his power. He was afraid of losing control. Really, that is not so unrelatable. When we choose to live from fear we hold so tight to our agenda that we can't see what God is doing. When we work to serve our own purposes we oppose the kingdom of God. When we let fear be master we are not willing to let Christ come as king and relinquish "our" kingdom. Instead, we hold on to it with all our might, doing whatever it takes to keep our grasp, not realizing that we really do not have control at all. Fear can be a gateway that leads us to unbelief, or an opportunity for us to slam the door shut, and choose to live from faith. By trusting God we put Him in control, and there is no greater peace and security than when Christ is king in us.

December 11ᵗʰ

BLESSED IS SHE WHO BELIEVED

LUKE 1:28-29, 34

And he came to her and said, "Greetings, O favored one, the Lord is with you!" But she was greatly troubled at the saying, and tried to discern what sort of greeting this might be.

And Mary said to the angel, "How will this be, since I am a virgin?"

It was a late summer day, calm and clear. My two year old son was napping, and the house was pleasantly quiet. I was sitting in my favorite armchair, penning advice to a friend, when I received a phone call from my doctor's office with startling news about my health. It was strange to take in the unexpected results, sandwiched in a good report. I'll never forget the sound of the nurse's voice, so calm, as though it were no big deal. My heart sank into my stomach. I knew what it meant; this news that had come so out of the blue would change my life forever. It took some time, but I worked through the fear that crept up on me in waves, until it ceased altogether. God had the final say on my life, and that's all that really mattered. I worked through the questions; the hard ones, the true ones, and I began to embrace the path before me with trust that I would find God's goodness on it.

The questions we ask reveal so much about our hearts. I love the exchange between the angel and Mary because it shows us how she responded to fear. Her situation was not so unlike my own. Change had come to her out of the blue. It took her by surprise, troubled her even, but we see through her questions a heart of belief. Even in the face of what was unknown to her, she did not waver in her faith. Difficulties come to all of us, but what will it reveal in our hearts when we are afraid? It is ok to have questions, but it is the motives of the heart behind the questions that is more important.

After Mary's encounter, Luke 1:39 says that she went with haste to go see Elizabeth. There is such good wisdom here. If you need to build up your faith, go recall what God has already done for you. Seek out others for their testimony. I have no doubt that Mary was seeking comfort, counsel, and encouragement by going to see Elizabeth. It must have built her faith to see that God had done in Elizabeth exactly as He said He would. When we read the beautiful exchange between these two women we do not see lives of worry or of fear, but hearts that are bursting with joy at the great things that God had done for them.

LUKE 1:45

And blessed is she who believed that there would be a fulfillment of what was spoken to her from the Lord.

December 12th

BETWEEN A ROCK
AND A HARD PLACE

LUKE 1:36-37

And behold, your relative Elizabeth in her old age has also conceived a son, and this is the sixth month with her who was called barren. For nothing will be impossible with God.

The story of Jesus' birth is such a gift. It shows us over and over again how God works through unlikely and even impossible ways. He loves to do marvelous things in people's lives because it reveals His glory, and dispels the doubt in our hearts. He came in such a way that worked through so many impossible things, because He wanted to give us hope. He reached through space, time, and impossibilities, just to redeem us back to Himself.

Are you in the middle of a difficult situation? Are the odds stacked against you? Believe it or not, you are in the perfect position to see God do amazing things. You are not at the end of your rope, you are at the beginning of the tipping point; the place where faith becomes miracles. Is it really such a wonder that the miracle maker came into this world through such unlikely ways? It should be no wonder either when He wants to come and work miracles in us through impossible odds. When God makes a way for us, it does not necessarily mean that He makes things work out the way we want them to. He knows what will work good in us, and for us. If we can trust Him in that, then we can put full faith in Him. We can't only have faith for what we want; we have to be willing to let God come and move the way He wants, even if it is in ways we never expected.

Think about Moses. He was in a position just like that, stuck between a rock and a hard place. An army on one side, a sea of impossibility on the other. I have passed through these situations time and again. In the momentary panic that often ensues as we assess the situation, we are faced with the choice of either letting the fear of the army overtake us, or stretching out our faith over the sea of impossibility before us for God to make a way. God can, and will always open a Red Sea for us, but we have to stretch out our faith first. It is an opportunity for us to exercise our faith, and by walking through the impossible we learn by doing. We learn through experience the strength of God's faithfulness in a way that is real and powerful. It is one thing to read about the greatness of God in somebody else's life, and it is another to walk through an impossible circumstance and see firsthand the mighty things God can do for you.

December 13th

FOCUS ON THE LORD

LUKE 1:46-55 THE MAGNIFICAT

*And Mary said, "My soul magnifies the Lord, and
my spirit rejoices in God my Savior, for he has
looked on the humble estate of his servant. For
behold, from now on all generations will call me
blessed; for he who is mighty has done great things
for me, and holy is his name. And his mercy is for
those who fear him from generation to generation.
He has shown strength with his arm; he has
scattered the proud in the thoughts of their hearts;
he has brought down the mighty from their thrones
and exalted those of humble estate; he has filled the
hungry with good things, and the rich he has sent
away empty. He has helped his servant Israel, in
remembrance of his mercy, as he spoke to our fathers,
to Abraham and to his offspring forever."*

Today's reflection is a simple one: to take a moment to focus in on all the good things that God has done for you. The word magnificat literally means to magnify, and that is exactly what Mary is doing in her song. She is taking out a magnifying glass and focusing in closely on the great things that God has done in her life. She is blessed, blown away by the awesomeness of who God is and the mighty things He has done for her. She is zooming in, taking a close look at His redemption, favor, power, majesty, mercy, strength, justice, and grace. He lifts the humble and fills the hungry; He took care of Mary and remembered His people Israel. He does amazing things. Let's take a moment to look into our own lives, to focus on the Lord with thanksgiving, and zoom in on the good and faithful things that He has done for us.

PSALM 100

Make a joyful noise to the Lord, all the earth! Serve the Lord with gladness! Come into his presence with singing! Know that the Lord, he is God! It is he who made us, and we are his; we are his people, and the sheep of his pasture. Enter his gates with thanksgiving, and his courts with praise! Give thanks to him; bless his name! For the Lord is good; his steadfast love endures forever, and his faithfulness to all generations.

PSALM 34:1-5

*I will bless the Lord at all times; his praise shall
continually be in my mouth. My soul makes its boast in
the Lord; let the humble hear and be glad. Oh, magnify
the Lord with me, and let us exalt his name together! I
sought the Lord, and he answered me and delivered me
from all my fears. Those who look to him are radiant,
and their faces shall never be ashamed.*

December 14th

WHEN GOD TAKES
AWAY OUR REPROACH

LUKE 1:24-25

*After these days his wife Elizabeth conceived, and
for five months she kept herself hidden, saying,
"Thus the Lord has done for me in the days when
he looked on me, to take away my reproach among
people."*

Barrenness is perhaps one of the hardest and most
lonely burdens to bear. I have been there, twice now,
aching with an insatiable desire, longing for God to
bless and open the womb. It has a way of making
you feel isolated, empty, and even forgotten. I often
blamed myself, and wondered if it was because I had
done something wrong or that I was being punished.
There couldn't possibly be a more inaccurate view of
God! Why we sometimes have to walk through the

sorrows we do, we don't always know, but one thing is absolutely certain: God is good, faithful, loving, and giving. He wants to heal, mend, and shower us with blessings. Healing doesn't always come in the form we want, or blessings for that matter, but sometimes, we do get to see the desires of our heart in our lifetime. Like Hannah, in 1 Samuel 1, who felt forgotten by God, and said, "He has remembered me," as she received the joy of a son. Elizabeth too. God did marvelous things for her even in her old age. He opened her womb and brought forth a prophet for His people. He took away her reproach and her shame.

LUKE 1:57

Now the time came for Elizabeth to give birth, and she bore a son. And her neighbors and relatives heard that the Lord had shown great mercy to her, and they rejoiced with her.

Is there a desire that has long burned in your heart? A lack that has left you feeling forgotten, even embarrassed? I want to encourage you today to not lose hope, that God has not forgotten you. Sometimes we feel as though God doesn't seem to want to bless us, and it is incredibly difficult to watch other people in our lives receive what our hearts have longed for. Don't lose heart. We don't always know the reason for the delay, but God can work much good in us, if we let Him. He really does have the best in mind for us.

Zechariah and Elizabeth's story is a beautiful one, and an encouraging reminder that God is never too late. His timing may not always make sense to us, but it is perfect. He is weaving a marvelous story, which we often don't understand, but the in's and out's are full of glory, and His goodness is interwoven at every step.

December 15th

FAITH LIFTS OUR BURDEN

LUKE 1:60-64

*But his mother answered, "No; he shall be called
John." And they said to her, "None of your relatives
is called by this name." And they made signs to
his father, inquiring what he wanted him to be
called. And he asked for a writing tablet and wrote,
"His name is John." And they all wondered. And
immediately his mouth was opened and his tongue
loosed, and he spoke, blessing God.*

For Zechariah, it must have felt like a great weight was
lifted from his shoulders. For months he had been held
silent, unable to utter a word. Even at the birth of his
son, he still could not speak. It wasn't until eight days
later that his burden was lifted and his mouth was
opened. There is something very significant here that I
think is often overlooked, but is key to understanding

the transformation that happened in this man's life. It was in Zechariah's *obedience* in naming their son John that he was finally able to speak. If you think about it, the Lord had opened Elizabeth's womb, but they had a choice to obey God's command in naming their son. By doing so, they were coming into alignment with God's plan, even though their family and friends did not understand and even questioned their decision.

The promise came, but it did not lift his burden. Zechariah's mouth was not opened until he responded in faith to what God was doing. I believe that God's timing in Zechariah's life was very strategic. Why did God wait till such an impossible time to bring such a blessing to this man? The impossibility itself was a grand invitation for Zechariah to grow in faith, and learn firsthand the strength of God's faithfulness. God cares very much about the condition of our hearts, and loves us enough to lead us through lessons of faith.

Doubt and fear are heavy burdens, weights that we were not meant to carry. I have been in circumstances in my life that were so daunting, I felt swallowed up by the impossibility of what I was facing. It wasn't until I chose to lean upon the faithfulness of God and believe all of what He said about my life that I found myself free of the doubt and fear. When I did, it was as though the greatest weight was lifted from me, and I could breathe again. When we respond in faith to God, He is able to lift the burdens of doubt and fear off of our lives, and we can move forward in the freedom and fullness of what God has for us. We may not always respond to fear the way we should, like Zechariah, but when the burden of doubt is lifted at the joy of the promise fulfilled, rejoice! Let the lesson sink in. See God's faithfulness, and let it transform your heart until you become so steadfast in the love of God that you are unmoved by outward circumstances.

December 16th

FAVOR IS FOR THE JOURNEY

ECCLESIASTES 3:1 NKJV
To everything there is a season, a time for every purpose under heaven.

Winter can be a time of such transition. Fall has come and gone, and with it the old is passing away. Winter comes to push us forward toward the new life ahead. On the surface it does not appear to be a season of growth, but that is not true. Beneath the surface, in all the silent, solemn peace, the earth is resting, waiting, regenerating for new life to come again. Every season has its purpose.

Favor has its purpose too. Like the winter season, we do not always see what favor is doing on the surface, but underneath a crucial work is going on, preparing a way for things to come. I don't know how, but somewhere along the line we got the idea that favor was about the end result, that favor was the blessing. We want favor because we want the end result of what we think favor will bring. That is not what favor is for. Favor is for the journey, not the destination.

God's promises are like the spring season, the time when we get to see the outworking, the fruition of what we have waited for. Like Zechariah, when the promise of the blessing comes to pass before our eyes, we can look back and see how favor was there at work all along. When the promise comes we often finally identify God's favor, and this is where I think we get the wrong idea about what the purpose of favor is. His favor does not arrive *with* the promise; His favor is what was there all along, working to *bring* the promise.

Favor is what makes a way for the promise to come. Like labor pains, favor opens up the way, though it is intensely painful at times. It is what gives us strength to get through seasons of transition. Favor is not for the end result of the blessing, but the gruesome process of getting there. If we can separate these concepts and really grasp what the purpose of favor is, we will have a much easier time identifying the favor that God has given us. With that understanding, we'll also have the comfort and joy of knowing that God is near and that He is for us, even when times are tough.

Favor was there for Mary and Joseph, helping them

through the difficulties of their journey. Favor was in Mary's womb, growing silently, unseen to the world. The hope of nations being knit together in darkness, until the light of the world would come forth and shine for all men. Jesus is the living proof of the Father's demonstrated delight towards us. What a marvelous gift!

LUKE 1:78-79

Because of the tender mercy of our God, whereby the sunrise shall visit us from on high to give light to those who sit in darkness and in the shadow of death, to guide our feet into the way of peace.

December 17th

LIVING FROM THE
SPIRIT OF GENEROSITY

LUKE 21:1-4

*Jesus looked up and saw the rich putting their gifts
into the offering box, and he saw a poor widow
put in two small copper coins. And he said, "Truly,
I tell you, this poor widow has put in more than
all of them. For they all contributed out of their
abundance, but she out of her poverty put in all she
had to live on."*

We live in a time where the holidays are just another
part of the hustle and bustle of our busy, modern day
lives, squeezing our pocketbooks, and adding to our
stress. Everywhere we turn there is the pressure to
keep up with the latest and the greatest. It is ironic
that for a culture that is so centered on material
things we still struggle to live generously. We are

constantly striving for more. We have more things than any other generation before us, and yet we are out of touch with the practice of giving. This reveals the truth that having more things does not make us more generous. Somehow, like favor, we've attached the idea of generosity to the idea of things.

This hit home for me more than ever during a Christmas when we did not have very much. I remember when I realized we would not be able to buy hardly anything. I felt so disappointed, until I began to feel convicted. This was not what Christmas was supposed to be about. I knew I had an opportunity before me to not only be happy with what I already had, but to not let it be an excuse to not be generous. This was the first year we decided "No debt allowed," when it came to Christmas. We would make do with whatever we had, and give from whatever we were able.

There are always ways to give generously, if we can be creative, because generosity is about blessing people, not just giving things. When we understand that favor is God's grace at work through the process, it releases our hearts to be generous, even through times of pain or lack. We do not have to be bogged down by barrenness, because we know God is at work to fulfill His promises, and we are on our way there. We can give from what we have, for grace begets graciousness.

There is something very moving, very transforming that happens when we give out of our lack, like the widow in Luke 21. There is something about giving generously when you have very little that helps remind you that we must be anchored to something much more real than what we physically see in this world. Being generous when we have very little also helps us to be generous when we have more. If we can't get past that stinginess when we don't have much, we won't have hearts to give when we have abundance. Just like favor, I believe that if we are faithful in being generous with what we have, God will give us more to be generous with. The best and truest generosity starts in the heart, and it works with whatever it has, a little or a lot.

December 18th

OUT OF THE ABUNDANCE OF THE HEART

PHILIPPIANS 2:3-4
Do nothing from selfish ambition or conceit, but in humility count others more significant than yourselves. Let each of you look not only to his own interests, but also to the interests of others.

Favor and generosity are like best friends — you will seldom see one without the other. When God looks on us with love He looks at us with favor, and with His favor is all the generosity of His heart for us. Generosity bespeaks of abundance, plentifulness, and kindness that has an open hand. So what cultivates a heart of generosity? First and foremost, identity. When we really begin to grasp the greatness of God's grace and favor it should transform us and the way we live. Generosity has to start somewhere. How can we be generous if we are bound by fear? How can we be generous if we are insecure and don't know who we are? We cannot. But when we know who we are in Christ, we have a place to begin from and to grow in, and who God is in us will begin to overflow in how we live.

When we understand the unearned favor that God has given us, we will live from the spirit of generosity. If we're not being generous it's because we have forgotten the undeserving grace and favor that God has extended to us. Just let that sink in for a moment. God gives us favor so that we can give favor to others. If we aren't looking to extend grace and favor to people, then we are not living from the heart of God. We can only give from what we have. The question is, what source are we tapping into? What source are we giving from? "Out of the abundance of the heart the mouth speaks." This is a deep, and yet profoundly simple principle. The fruit of our lives will show what we are rooted in. If we do not habitually live by grace and generosity towards others, then we need to take a look at what we are rooted in.

Another important way we can cultivate a heart of generosity is by honor and humility. In humility we should view others with the same grace that God has given us, and "count others more significant than ourselves." We show honor when we bestow favor on others by being gracious in the way we look at people and in putting their interests above our own. A gracious spirit always lends to honoring others and a heart that is generous. Generosity is favor which gives above and beyond what is due, and what greater reminder is there than Christmas itself, when God gave us a gift greater than anything we could have ever deserved.

LUKE 6:45

The good person out of the good treasure of his heart produces good, and the evil person out of his evil treasure produces evil, for out of the abundance of the heart his mouth speaks.

December 19ᵗʰ

FAVOR IS FOR THE KINGDOM

ESTHER 4:14

For if you keep silent at this time, relief and deliverance will rise for the Jews from another place, but you and your father's house will perish. And who knows whether you have not come to the kingdom for such a time as this?

Esther was a beautiful young woman, orphaned and living with her uncle. She was taken into the king's palace as a candidate for queen, and being brought into custody, she found great favor with Hegai, the man in charge (Esther 2:9). He blessed her abundantly with gifts, and advanced her, and with his advice she won favor in the eyes of all who saw her (Esther 2:15). When it was her turn to come before the king, verse 17 says he loved her more than all the women and that she won grace and favor in his sight more than anyone else. He chose her as queen and put a crown on her head. When a plot was devised to annihilate the Jews, Esther risked her own life to go before the king, and with the favor that was extended to her, she saved her people.

Esther had favor because of who she was, not because of what she had. God didn't set her up as queen so she could enjoy the high life; He placed her there so that she could be an extension of grace and favor to His people. Have you ever been encouraged when you were blessed by someone else's favor? When they extended their favor to you, even though you did not deserve it? That is what favor is for. It is for extending grace, and by doing so we become conduits of God's kingdom. God gives us favor because He loves us, and He cannot help but delight in us. We are made in His image, and as children of God we should have the same heart for other people that God has for us.

The devil wants us to believe the lie that we are disqualified based on what we have, or don't have. You might find yourself without much, and the enemy will have you to believe that somehow *you* are less, or that because you don't have many resources that you can't make a difference. His mission is to make you afraid, like the steward in the parable of the talents, and get you to do nothing when God wants to use you and the favor He has given you for His kingdom.

Esther's uncle, Mordecai, warned her that if she did nothing her position would not save her, and that she would die along with her people. With great courage she was faithful with what she had been given, and it made a difference in the lives of thousands of people. God gives us each favor for a purpose and a reason. Let's be faithful with whatever it is He has given us — you never know when that favor might lead you to come before kings to be an extension of His grace and favor to others.

THE WISE MEN'S GIFTS

MATTHEW 2:10-11

When they saw the star, they rejoiced exceedingly with great joy. And going into the house they saw the child with Mary his mother, and they fell down and worshiped him. Then, opening their treasures, they offered him gifts, gold and frankincense and myrrh.

Some time after Jesus was born, wise men came from the east, seeking the one who had been born king of the Jews. The journey they took was no doubt long, costly, and time-consuming. Why would they have traveled so far, just to bring gifts to a small child? We can only guess how much they knew about who Jesus was and what He would become. They were well-educated, wealthy men, even astrologers. They knew the stars, and they knew the scripture. They would have been respected men of science, and yet they came quoting the prophet, recognizing that a great ruler had been born. They came prepared to worship Him, bringing invaluable gifts fit for royalty, or one destined to rule. Why did they bring Him gold, frankincense, and myrrh?

Gold: the metal of kings, it acknowledged His right to rule. They recognized that this was no ordinary child, but that Jesus was king. He may have only been a child, but they came with bent knee. Gold represents Christ's Lordship, that He is King of Kings.

Frankincense: an incense used for worship, fitting for Jesus, our High Priest. Frankincense was used in the temple for worship and to anoint the priests of Israel. They recognized Jesus as High Priest and worthy of praise, which is why when they saw Him, they fell down and worshiped Him.

Myrrh: an anointing oil, a gift of faith to honor the sacrifice to be given. It was used to embalm the dead. Not a usual gift you would bring a person at the beginning of their life, but this bespoke of the reason He had come into the world: to be a sacrifice, a ransom for our sins.

Thank you Jesus for being our King, our Priest, and our Salvation. Let us recognize all that He is, and may our hearts lovingly enthrone Him this Christmas!

Born a king on Bethlehem's plain,
Gold I bring to crown Him again,
King forever, ceasing never
Over us all to reign.

Frankincense to offer have I.
Incense owns a Deity nigh.
Prayer and praising all men raising,
Worship Him, God on high.

Myrrh is mine: its bitter perfume
Breathes a life of gathering gloom.
Sorrowing, sighing, bleeding dying,
Sealed in the stone-cold tomb.

Glorious now behold Him arise,
King and God and Sacrifice.
Alleluia, alleluia!
Sounds through the earth and skies.

- We Three Kings

December 21st

A LIGHT FOR REVELATION, PART I

MATTHEW 2:1-2 NIV

After Jesus was born in Bethlehem in Judea, during
the time of King Herod, Magi from the east came
to Jerusalem and asked, "Where is the one who has
been born king of the Jews? We saw his star when it
rose and have come to worship him."

The traditional nativity scene is one that has been
stamped in our minds from early childhood. Mary and
Joseph huddled together, leaning over a baby lying in
straw. The stable and the shepherds, the animals and
the Christmas star. The three wise men carrying their
gifts, riding in on a string of camels. We've seen it
again and again, from movies to Christmas cards and
pageants. It's a sort of condensed version of Biblical
truth and the inaccuracies of tradition, all bundled
together into one scene. I can definitely say it is hard

to lose this image, even when we approach the Word and read the full account ourselves. We walk away missing the details of the story when we have been given such a condensed version of it over and over again.

The journey of the magi represents something of such great importance, though it is often overlooked. Who were they, why had they come so far, and what does their journey have to do with us? We've already looked at the powerful representation of the gifts that they brought to Jesus, now let's look at how God was using these men from the east to speak a very important message. They had come a very, very long way, these magi. Driven in their search for something of more value than the great gifts they carried. All of us have been, or are at some point on the journey of searching. In our hearts is a great discontent; we are searching for something of value, something to define purpose and meaning in our lives.

We commonly call them the wise men because they were most likely men of high education; astronomy, philosophy, science, perhaps even priests of ancient Media or Persia. They may have been advisors to the kings of their day, being men of great influence. With that, they would have had great wealth as well. When we look at the Old Testament, from Daniel to Esther, we know that God's people had been around and influenced the areas where they probably came from, so it is not completely surprising that they had knowledge of the scriptures. They were well versed in them. They knew the stars. They too, like the Jews, were watching and waiting for the coming Messiah, though they were of a much different religious sort. The more we know of them, the stranger it seems that they went so far out of their way to search for a king who was so outside the spectrum of their own culture.

They would have been the kind of people that already had all that they needed. Why then would they embark on such a great adventure? It would have cost a fortune, and would have taken many months. Like Mary and Joseph, their friends and family probably misunderstood the point of such a crazy pursuit. Something had moved their hearts enough that they found purpose and joy in counting the cost to go. They left their homes, their culture, their people, and their religion, to search for a king who had only just been born. A king whose reign was so important to them, they gave up everything to go find him and worship him.

December 22nd

A LIGHT FOR REVELATION, PART II

LUKE 2:10
And the angel said to them, "Fear not, for behold, I bring you good news of great joy that will be for all the people."

LUKE 2:29-32
"Lord, now you are letting your servant depart in peace, according to your word; for my eyes have seen your salvation that you have prepared in the presence of all peoples, a light for revelation to the Gentiles, and for glory to your people Israel."

The magi from the east had a purpose and a vision that was so much bigger than themselves, that they left everything they knew to go and search for it. The extravagance of the gifts they carried were nothing to the value of what they were searching for. Think about it, why would they have brought such costly gifts with them if they did not know the purpose of their journey? They saw His star rise in the east, and they were going after the great king.

When the wise men arrive in Jerusalem asking, "Where is he who has been born king of the Jews?" We actually see that perhaps the star did not guide them the whole way, contrary to popular belief. If it had, they wouldn't have needed to stop and ask for directions. They were truly on a journey of faith. All of a sudden Matthew 2:9-10 makes so much more sense, "After listening to the king, they went on their way. And behold, the star that they had seen when it rose went before them until it came to rest over the place where the child was. When they saw the star, they rejoiced exceedingly with great joy." God had not left them hanging, their journey was not in vain! They celebrated because they had found what their hearts were seeking.

The creative ways of God amaze me, and how He will go to whatever lengths it takes to draw us to Himself. These wise men had an encounter with God that was no doubt life altering. They also represent something very important; that Jesus had not just come for the Jews, but for all people. I am so thankful that God had a plan for the all of us! Long before the wise men came, the angels had echoed this plan when they proclaimed it to the shepherds the night that Jesus was born. Good news had come for everyone.

When Jesus was presented in the temple, a man name Simeon took Him in his arms, and with a blessing proclaimed that God had prepared salvation for all people, a light of revelation for the Gentiles, and glory to His people Israel. These beautiful words were embodied in the wise men's arrival, and their example is before us. We too can count the cost and go after God no matter what it takes. God has made a way for all of us, and we have the invitation to respond to Him with our whole hearts.

December 23rd

A Name Above Every Name

JOHN 1:1-5, 14

*In the beginning was the Word, and the Word was
with God, and the Word was God. He was in the
beginning with God. All things were made through
him, and without him was not any thing made that
was made. In him was life, and the life was the
light of men. The light shines in the darkness, and
the darkness has not overcome it.*

*And the Word became flesh and dwelt among us,
and we have seen his glory, glory as of the only Son
from the Father, full of grace and truth.*

The Word became flesh. All of God wrapped up in
an infant, taking the form of a servant and being
born in the likeness of man. It seems impossible that
something so big could be wrapped up in something

so small, or that time itself could even contain in a moment of history the one who spoke it into existence by the word of His mouth. The Word was God Himself, moving and creating. The Word that spoke the universe into existence and set time in motion, became flesh. Is there any wonder that there is so much power in the name of Jesus?

There is power in the name of Jesus because all of who God is, and all His creative power is embodied in Him. He is the light that the darkness could not overcome. At His name the sick are healed. At His name the dead are raised. At His name the lost are saved. He is the miracle maker because He is the one who creates. He is not bound by physical laws, because everything that has been created was made by Him. It is as marvelous as it is mysterious. It gives hope because we have a God with whom nothing is impossible. In that moment, as a baby in a manger, a great light had come to men; to bring hope, to bring salvation. The name above every name.

What child is this, who, laid to rest,
On Mary's lap is sleeping?

Whom angels greet with anthems sweet,
While shepherds watch are keeping?

This, this is Christ the King,

Whom shepherds guard and angels sing:

    Haste, haste to bring Him laud,
    The babe, the son of Mary.

Why lies He in such mean estate,
    Where ox and donkeys are feeding?
Good Christians, fear, for sinners here
    The silent Word is pleading.
Nails, spears shall pierce him through,
    The cross he bore for me, for you.
    Hail, hail the Word made flesh,
    The Babe, the Son of Mary.

So bring him incense, gold, and myrrh,
    Come, peasant, king, to own him.
The King of kings salvation brings,
    Let loving hearts enthrone him.
    Raise, raise a song on high,
    The virgin sings her lullaby
    Joy, joy for Christ is born,
    The babe, the Son of Mary.

- What Child Is This

December 24th

THE PRINCE OF PEACE

ISAIAH 9:2, 6
The people who walked in darkness have seen a great light; those who dwelt in a land of deep darkness, on them has light shone.

For to us a child is born, to us a son is given; and the government shall be upon his shoulder, and his name shall be called Wonderful Counselor, Mighty God, Everlasting Father, Prince of Peace.

MATTHEW 1:23
"Behold, the virgin shall conceive and bear a son, and they shall call his name Immanuel" (which means, God with us).

Rejoice, rejoice! God is with us! We have a great High Priest, our Prince of Peace. He is not far away, hidden behind the veil. Jesus went in for us and was our sacrifice. He has redeemed us to Himself, and the veil has been torn. All that separated us has been removed. He is our Immanuel, He is with us. Isn't this such good news? There was a time when only a priest could go in to the holy of holies, to make amends and to worship. When Jesus redeemed us with His great sacrifice, the veil in the temple was torn in two. That veil represented a separation between us and God, but with Jesus' blood we are separated no more. We can come into the holy of holies, boldly before the throne of grace, and have relationship with the Father. Jesus is our Prince of Peace, He is mighty, and He has bought us with a price. God is not some *thing* we worship, stale and cold. He is not silent, angry, or far off. He is near. He is *someone*, and He beckons us with love into His presence.

Hebrews 6:19-20 NKJV

This hope we have as an anchor of the soul, both sure and steadfast, and which enters the Presence behind the veil, where the forerunner has entered for us, even Jesus, having become High Priest forever according to the order of Melchizedek.

He made a way for us. He made peace for us. He is our anchor of hope. Thank you Jesus!

O ye beneath life's crushing load,
Whose forms are bending low,
Who toil along the climbing way
With painful steps and slow;
Look now, for glad and golden hours
Come swiftly on the wing;
Oh rest beside the weary road
And hear the angels sing.
For lo! The days are hastening on,
By prophets seen of old,
When with the ever-circling years
Shall come the time foretold,
When the new heaven and earth shall own
The Prince of Peace, their King,
And the whole world send back the song
Which now the angels sing.

- IT CAME UPON A MIDNIGHT CLEAR

December 25th

THE PERFECT GIFT

JOHN 14:27

Peace I leave with you; my peace I give to you. Not as the world gives do I give to you. Let not your hearts be troubled, neither let them be afraid.

Christmas Day has come again, and with it, the childlike excitement that stirs our hearts to wonder. So much of the year is filled with the bleak business of living, but we were meant for so much more. We meant for wonder. When I think of what it means to wonder I imagine the face of a child on Christmas morning, full of excitement and hope for what is ahead. I believe that God wants to draw us to Himself, and fill our hearts with fresh awe at His goodness, and to renew our courage and our hope for what lies ahead. He has good gifts for every heart that searches for Him. It takes but a moment to come away from the noise and celebration, a moment to connect. There is something in the silence, if we can take the time to listen and steady our hearts to hear it; a peace in the quiet. Peace that spreads through the soul like a warm stream of light, brightening every bit of space and illuminating all the shadows of fear. Hope is awakened like wonder in the heart of a child. The gifts of Christmas were meant to fill us with the light of joy and the sound of hope, flooding and filling our hearts, making all the sorrows of the year recede into memory. What a beautiful gift, "My peace I give to you," that our hearts would not be troubled, that we would know that we have nothing to fear. Only God's favor could give us such a wonderful and perfect gift.

O little town of Bethlehem,
How still we see thee lie!

Above your deep and dreamless sleep,
The silent stars go by.

Yet in thy dark streets shineth
The everlasting Light,

The hopes and fears of all the years,
Are met in thee tonight.

O morning stars, together
Proclaim thy holy birth

And praises sing to God, the King,
And peace to men on earth.

For Christ is born of Mary,
And gathered all above,

While mortals sleep, the angels keep
Their watch of wondering love.

How silently, how silently,
The wondrous Gift is giv'n!

So God imparts to human hearts
The blessings of His heaven.

No ear may hear His coming,
But in this world of sin,

Where meek souls will receive Him still,
The dear Christ enters in.

O holy Child of Bethlehem,
Descend to us, we pray;

Cast out our sins and enter in,
Be born to us today.

We hear the Christmas angels
The great glad tidings tell:

Oh, come to us, abide with us,
Our Lord Emmanuel!

- O LITTLE TOWN OF BETHLEHEM

Made in the USA
Monee, IL
27 August 2020

39365339R00073